essentials

essentials liefern aktuelles Wissen in konzentrierter Form. Die Essenz dessen, worauf es als „State-of-the-Art" in der gegenwärtigen Fachdiskussion oder in der Praxis ankommt. *essentials* informieren schnell, unkompliziert und verständlich

- als Einführung in ein aktuelles Thema aus Ihrem Fachgebiet
- als Einstieg in ein für Sie noch unbekanntes Themenfeld
- als Einblick, um zum Thema mitreden zu können

Die Bücher in elektronischer und gedruckter Form bringen das Fachwissen von Springerautor*innen kompakt zur Darstellung. Sie sind besonders für die Nutzung als eBook auf Tablet-PCs, eBook-Readern und Smartphones geeignet. *essentials* sind Wissensbausteine aus den Wirtschafts-, Sozial- und Geisteswissenschaften, aus Technik und Naturwissenschaften sowie aus Medizin, Psychologie und Gesundheitsberufen. Von renommierten Autor*innen aller Springer-Verlagsmarken.

More information about this series at https://link.springer.com/bookseries/13088

Timo Sedelmeier · Olaf Kühne ·
Corinna Jenal

Foodscapes

 Springer VS

Timo Sedelmeier
Forschungsbereich Geographie
Universität Tübingen
Tübingen, Germany

Olaf Kühne
Forschungsbereich Geographie
University of Tübingen
Tübingen, Germany

Corinna Jenal
Forschungsbereich Geographie
Universität Tübingen
Tübingen, Germany

ISSN 2197-6708   ISSN 2197-6716 (electronic)
essentials
ISBN 978-3-658-36705-3   ISBN 978-3-658-36706-0 (eBook)
https://doi.org/10.1007/978-3-658-36706-0

Translation from the German language edition: essentials_Foodscapes/Nahrungslandschaften by Timo Sedelmeier, Olaf Kühne, Corinna Jenal, ©Der/die Herausgeber bzw. der/die Autor(en), exklusiv lizenziert durch Springer Fachmedien Wiesbaden GmbH, ein Teil von Springer Nature 2021. Published by Springer Fachmedien Wiesbaden. All Rights reserved.

Responsible Editor: Dr. Cori Antonia Mackrodt
This Springer VS imprint is published by the registered company Springer Fachmedien Wiesbaden GmbH part of Springer Nature.
The registered company address is: Abraham-Lincoln-Str. 46, 65189 Wiesbaden, Germany

What You Can Find in This *essential*

- An introduction to *essential* tenets of 'foodscapes', from their beginnings to new approaches.
- The presentation of the conceptual history of 'landscape' and scientific research perspectives (essentialism, positivism and constructivism).
- A differentiation of constructivist perspectives on 'foodscapes' with a focus on social constructivist and discourse theory approaches.
- An illustration of 'foodscapes' using selected case studies including applied research methods.
- An illustration of the relevance of food geography and other potential research perspectives.

Contents

1 Introduction 1

2 On the Concept of Landscape 3

3 Food Geography—Histories of a Forming Geographical
Subdiscipline 11

4 The Multidimensionality of the Concept of 'foodscapes' 15

5 The Impact of Political or Social Systems on 'foodscapes' 21

6 'Poverty Foodscapes'—Two Case Studies 25
  6.1 The Tafel food bank 25
  6.2 Baton Rouge—Plank Road, from historical and spatial
      contextualization of a 'poverty foodscape' to its
      phenomenological experience 27

7 Conclusion 33

References 37

Introduction

The name of the subject 'foodscapes' is formed by a composite of the words 'food' as well as '-skape'. If different 'semantic yards' (Hard, 1969) of '-skape' and 'landscape' are disregarded, 'foodscapes' is used to denote a synthesis of spatially differentiated availabilities and productions of food. From this understanding of the term it becomes clear that 'foodscapes' can be understood both from a constructivist perspective (as a conceptual notion, synopsis, synthesis) and from a positivist perspective, at the level of 'physical-material spaces', the distribution of 'something', in this case, the production, distribution as well as accessibility (here in the sense of physical-spatial, not, for instance, social distances) in a space conceived as a container (cf: Adema, 2010). The term 'foodscape' emerged in the mid-1990s (Yasmeen, 1996) in the context of the scientific study of social and spatial inequalities in public health and food systems. (Vonthron et al., 2020). However, issues of food production, its distribution, marketing, as well as consumption have a history that dates back to the early nineteenth century in geography and its neighboring disciplines. They are characterized by the fact that the focus of scientific observation has increasingly shifted towards consumption in recent decades. Closely linked to this development are also changing notions of space and landscape. As a starting point for our reflections on 'foodscapes', we therefore outline the changing understanding of landscape (Chap. 2). Building on this, the development of food geography into an independent sub-discipline of human geography will be presented (Chap. 3). Within the 'geography of food', the study of 'foodscapes' has gained in significance in the last two decades—a circumstance we want to take into account with this *Essential* by outlining the guidelines of this development and the most important fields of research—without claiming to be exhaustive (Chap. 4). The development of 'foodscapes' depends on a variety of factors, including not only economic, social and environmental, but also political ones. Therefore, in the fifth

T. Sedelmeier et al., *Foodscapes*, essentials,
https://doi.org/10.1007/978-3-658-36706-0_1

chapter, we turn to different political systems and illustrate their socio-spatial effects by means of two examples, which we subsume under the term 'poverty foodscapes' (Chap. 6).

This volume about 'foodscapes' is a translation of a German-language book. Thus, in addition to the international state of research, the current discussions in the German-speaking world about foodscapes and landscape are reflected. This gives international readers the opportunity to engage with discussions that would otherwise have less international presence. This also applies to approaches that were developed in the German-speaking world and are not yet part of the international mainstream, such as the neopragmatic landscape theory.

On the Concept of Landscape

The second part of the word 'foodscapes' refers to 'landscape' (or -scape), i.e. to a spatial synopsis of 'something'. In this chapter we deal with the genesis of this mode of synopsis and the current meaning of the term 'landscape', which will be the basis for the further remarks on 'foodscapes'. In the following, we will deal in particular with the development of the German concept of landscape. There are two reasons for this: first, it has the longest history here; second, this understanding became dominant in international terminology from the end of the nineteenth century. In order to indicate that in the presentation of the development of the German-language concept of landscape we are referring to this specific concept (not the understanding of the English-language concept of landscape) we mark this with the use of the German word "Landschaft". On this basis, we also address landscape concepts that have developed outside the German-speaking world.

As a result of its history going back to the Middle Ages, the concept of landscape has developed -as already mentioned – a large 'semantic yard'(Hard, 1969). In the course of the history of the term, new connotations were added, the term became more diverse and thus also less unambiguous. This development makes it versatile, but also necessary to explain the conceptual understandings used, if it is not to have a merely ornamental character. In this respect, this chapter is first devoted to a concise history of the term, from which it becomes clear what conceptual references the term 'landscape' has for research on the production, distribution, and accessibility of and to food. In addition, current theoretical approaches to landscape research are presented and, finally, the understanding of landscape used in the following is derived.

The development of the German concept of landscape in recent years has become the subject of numerous scholarly reappraisals (for example, at: Berr & Kühne, 2020; Berr & Schenk, 2019; Müller, 1977; Schenk, 2013; Trepl, 2012),

T. Sedelmeier et al., *Foodscapes*, essentials,
https://doi.org/10.1007/978-3-658-36706-0_2

insofar the lines of development will only be roughly outlined in the following. 'Landschaft' represents in Germanic languages a verbal abstract (similar to: *skapi-, *skapja- and *skafti-) derived from other numerous -skapjan ('schaften') (as also Mannschaft (team), Vorstandschaft (management), Freundschaft (friendship) etc.). These -schaft-abstracts were (and are) characterized by a unified meaning spectrum, a synopsis of gestalt, form, constitution, nature, condition, and manner.

The beginnings of the concept of landscape can be traced back in German to the early ninth century (Gruenter, 1975 [1953]). In Old High German, 'Landschaft' referred to something "which in the vast majority of cases has the quality of a larger settlement area" (Müller, 1977, p. 6) As a derivative of descriptions of persons or groups of persons, 'landscape' also encompassed a basic meaning of the behaviors common in a particular area. 'Landscape' also denoted the social norms of the inhabitants living in that area. However, this did not establish a direct link to physical space. An expansion of the understanding took place in the course of the twelfth century: 'Landschaft' became a political-legal concept of space, it was understood as a political subspace of a larger political unit (Müller, 1977). It also included the politically capable (i.e. not the unfree) of a region in the form of the "representatives of the 'whole Landschaft'" (Hard, 1977, p. 14). In the High Middle Ages, 'Landschaft' was concretized: 'Landschaft' was understood as the space dominated and cultivated by a city (Müller, 1977). This conceptual meaning was later extended in the dichotomous separation into 'Kulturlandschaft' (cultural landscape, i.e. the high medieval understanding of 'Landschaft') and 'Naturlandschaft' (natural landscape, uncultivated area which lay beyond the cultivated 'Landschaft' in the Middle Ages).

'Landschaft' acquired a new component of meaning in the Renaissance: starting from Dutch (landscape) painting, the word acquired an aesthetic meaning, such as the Anglo-Saxon 'scenery' (Antrop, 2019; Büttner, 2006). Thus, the 'double character' of the term in German, which still exists today, came into being: First, 'Landschaft' denotes the arrangement of material objects, beyond the local level of observation; second, 'Landschaft' also denotes the synthesis of such objects in an aesthetic synopsis. This de-differentiation of object- and meta-level is characteristic for the understanding of landscape in the German-speaking world, for instance in comparison to other European languages. Other languages, such as English or French, focus more strongly on the aesthetic dimension; an understanding similar to German, is found in Hungarian (cf. et al. Drexler, 2013). The concept of 'Landschaft' experienced a special charge in German Romanticism, "in that mythological and historical contents were absorbed into an expanded concept of 'Landschaft'" (Hohl, 1977, p. 45; cf. Piepmeier,

1980). Thus, for the Romantic painters—Caspar David Friedrich (1774–1840) was particularly influential—painting became an expression of "the inner and moral and religious constitution of the artist" (Büttner, 2006, p. 262).'Landschaft' experienced a sacral significance. Scientifically, in the eighteenth century, a non-aesthetic understanding of landscape, going back to the late medieval, in the sense of area or territory, was still handed down, which was replaced by the phrase attributed to Alexander von Humboldt of 'total character of an area of the earth (Hard, 1969; Schmithüsen, 1968). The Biedermeier period was also reflected in the modification of the understanding of 'Landschaft': it became a symbol of humanity. This was threatened by the development of civilization as well as by an increasing economic—technically mediated—utilization of 'Landschaft'. Accordingly, the expansion of cities, the construction of industrial plants, and the 'mechanization of the land' were at the center of criticism (Kortländer, 1977). Thus 'Landschaft' became the medium of social criticism. This tradition is also updated to this day, on the level of objects, for example in the context of the material manifestations of the energy transition (such as wind turbines). Additionally, this tradition is also continued in the more abstract engagements with the thematic field of 'landscape and justice', which is constitutive for the concept of 'foodscapes'. At the end of the nineteenth century—in rejection of the processes and structures of social modernization—the 'pre-modern rural landscape' was idealized as home. In order To protect it, the 'Heimatschutzbewegung' was founded (Eisel, 1982; Lekan & Zeller, 2005). Thus, the idea of an "always individual[ed] and organic[ed] harmony of culture and nature" emerged, which "can then be read in the landscape" (Körner, 2006a: 6). A conception of 'cultural landscape' emerged, whose material appearance was the expression of a 'being' that was produced by the mutual imprinting of (regional) nature and culture that had taken place over generations. This variety of interpretation and evaluation of 'Landschaft' shaped (more or less unreflected) the understanding of 'Landschaft' in German geography (especially in the form of 'Landschaftskunde') at the change from the 19th to the twentieth century. This understanding, as numerous people from abroad studied or earned doctorates in Germany or went abroad from Germany, became embedded in numerous research traditions beyond German jargon (as in the United States, Japan, China; Denevan & Mathewson, 2009; Küchler & Wang 2009; Ueda, 2010). After Nazi Germany's attempt to establish the principle of Deutsche Kulturlandschaft' ('German cultural landscape') in the physical spaces of the occupied states of East-Central Europe (especially Poland), the term was given a more scientific character in the 1960s. In contrast, it was largely eradicated from (West) German human geography (in the context of the Kiel Geographers' Day in 1969). Only in the context of the physical side effects of economic structural change (keyword: 'old industrialization') and the 'constructivist turn' did the term experience a certain renaissance (among many: Höfer & Vicenzotti, 2013; Jenal, 2019; Kühne, 2016; Schönwald, 2015). These remarks also show (rather implicitly) changes of scientific perspectives to and on ''. These different understandings will now be explicitly addressed in the following.

As with the history of concepts, a number of survey works have been published on landscape theory in recent decades. These exhibit varying degrees of detail as well as different theoretical and thematic perspectives (for example, at: Bourassa, 1991; Kühne, 2018a, 2019a; Winchester et al., 2003; Wylie, 2007). Therefore, a brief overview is sufficient here to present the *essential* features of the landscape theoretical approaches mentioned above, the essentialist, the positivist, and the constructivist (a connection of landscape to scientific theories can be found in detail in: Kühne & Berr, 2021).

Essentialism (from Latin '*essentia*' = essence) is characterized by the belief "that the goal of science is to reveal entities and to describe them by means of definitions" (Popper, 2003[1945], p. 40). The essentialist understanding of landscape accordingly assumes that the material appearances of a 'landscape' (not merely in the sense of the traditional German landscape understanding) are an expression of its 'essence'. This is characterized by a mutual formation of a regional culture and nature lasting over generations. Thus, it is assumed that a) the essence (the reason or the 'underlying' of 'existence', facticity or 'Dasein') determines the form of the 'landscape' and—beyond that—a distinction is made between b) the "things possessing necessary properties that constitute their essence" (Chilla et al., 2015, p. 15) and those that are merely accidental, to be found in a 'landscape'. Thus, there is a fundamental distinction between *essential* (*essential, necessary*) properties (here of landscape) and accidental (accidental, contingent) properties. The *essential* properties of a thing (here landscape) made it "what it is, while the accidental properties have no such significance for the thing's existence" (Albert, 2005, p. 44). The task of (landscape) researchers is—from this perspective—accordingly not to investigate attributions, interpretations and valuations. The 'essence of the landscape' (in the singular, of course) must rather be "sought and founded in the object itself" (Lautensach, 1973, p. 24). Since from this perspective landscape is regarded as a "quasi organismic whole with special characteristics", which has "an unalterable intrinsic value and an identity of its own " (Gailing & Leibenath, 2012, p. 97),, strict norms are formulated for dealing with 'landscape'. Everything that is understood as an expression of the 'essence of the landscape' is to be preserved, whereaseverything that is 'accidental' is to be avoided. Historic land forms, farmhouse forms, road surfaces, etc.

are considered '*essential*', while row house settlements, large-scale land clearing, especially the functionalist 'global building style' are not.

The notion of science as 'discoverer' of an 'essence' hidden behind appearances—in this case landscape—is rejected by positivist landscape research. Landscape, from this perspective, is an object to be grasped empirically by measuring, weighing, and counting, and—broken down into individual phenomena—can be analyzed. The positivist concept of landscape follows the modern understanding of science in that "'collected' observations are inductively generalized by the mind" (Eisel, 2009, p. 18). 'Landscape' in this understanding is understood as "real reality" (Schultze, 1973, p. 203) as a container, which is 'filled' with different elements. These elements relate to each other—in a mathematically determinable way. Thus, landscape—in this perspective—can be divided into different levels (in Geographic Information Systems: layers), in which climate, vegetation, settlements, etc. are recorded, making them accessible to computer-aided modeling (cf. Tilley, 1997). On the basis of positivistic landscape research, norms for the design of the materially understood 'landscape' are hardly possible, after all, this is oriented towards the analysis of interrelationships (Kühne, 2019c).

If the constitutive level of landscape for an essentialist understanding lies in its 'essence', which is expressed through 'appearances' and must be identified by landscape-related science, from the positivist understanding, landscape is understood as an object whose individual appearances are first observed and measured, then represented—structured by layers—and finally generalized inductively. Even if constructivist approaches differ in terms of their scientific-theoretical justification and their focus on different processes, they are generally based on the view that the constitutive level of landscape lies in social or individual construction processes. Thus, social constructivist landscape theory focuses on the question of how social ideas about landscape are conveyed in the process of socialization, how these ideas are internalized, how one's own ideas about landscape are developed, for example in the form of preferences, and how innovative ideas are socially negotiated. In addition, it deals with how material objects are symbolically charged and thus fulfill social functions. It also explores the question of the significance and impact of power in these processes (Cosgrove, 1984; Greider & Garkovich, 1994; Kühne, 2008). The question of social distribution of power is addressed even more strongly in the perspective of discourse-theoretical landscape research: Discourses here "regulate the way in which a topic can be meaningfully talked about and reflected upon" (Hall, 2001, p. 72). Discourses nonetheless emerge in conflict: "By making certain discourses hegemonic and others marginal, certain truths and ultimately certain social realities are produced"

(Glasze & Mattissek, 2009, p. 12). Accordingly, discourse-analytic landscape research examines the different discourses about landscape (for example, as 'historically evolved' vs. 'modern'), the competitions among them, how they strive for hegemonicity and strive to secure this hegemonicity (see e.g. Leibenath & Otto, 2013; Weber, 2019). Less interested in questions of unequal power structures is the radical constructivist landscape research. Following Niklas Luhmann (1986) it addresses questions of how social subsystems, such as politics, economics, science, etc., construct landscape in different ways. This construction takes place, for example, with regard to the questions of how landscape is used as a medium to generate power, to earn money or to generate knowledge that leads to reputation. From this perspective, one can also address the question of how the expansion of mass media (especially in social networks such as Facebook) moral communication resonates with the other subsystems of society (Kühne, 2019b; Kühne et al., 2021).

In recent years, landscape theory research has increasingly discussed approaches that seek to bridge a clear separation between object and subject. However, these have not (yet) found significant expression in the current state of discussion regarding 'foodscapes'. First, there is a return to phenomenology, which deals with the individual experience of landscape, whereby researchers become narrators of their experiences of and with landscape (Tilley, 1997; Tuan, 1989). In actor-network theory, 'landscape' is formed from social, technical, and natural entities and factors as principally equal nodes of networking processes (Allen, 2011; Latour, 1996, 1997; Latour & Roßler, 2007 [2005]). These are treated by "actor-network theory not as explanans but as explananda" (Schulz-Schaeffer, 2000, p. 188). The assemblage theory focuses (starting from a constructivist position) on how material things can (socially) act (Müller, 2015; van Wezemael & Loepfe, 2009). Another way of integrating material aspects, individual consciousness and social contents is taken by neopragmatic landscape and regional geographic research: Under a social constructivist framework, a triangulation of data, methods, persons and especially theories, as outlined in the foregoing, is carried out here for the investigation of complex (spatial) phenomena, that are derived and justified from concrete questions (Kühne, 2018b; Kühne & Jenal, 2021).

Aware of these different theoretical approaches, we understand landscape as a social pattern of synthesis, interpretation and evaluation actualizing individual construction. In this construction, material objects are linked in a relational arrangement and meanings are attributed to them. This understanding of landscape is open to different scientific theoretical perspectives, methodological approaches, researcher perspectives and data, within a (social)constructivist framework. In short, our understanding of 'landscape' can be understood as 'neopragmatic'. In the following, based on what has been outlined about the formation of spatial syntheses (here: landscapes) on the one hand, and the science-theoretical framings that have been presented here in relation to landscape on the other hand, we will present the development of the geographical engagement with food up to the development of the concept of 'foodscapes'.

Recommended reading:

- Trepl (2012): A cultural-historical overview of understandings of landscape, especially in the German-speaking world.
- Kühne (2019a): An up-to-date, English-language, concise introduction to currently discussed theoretical approaches as well as current challenges in dealing with landscape.
- Wylie (2007): A now-classic introduction to landscape theory, with a particular focus on discussions in the Anglo-Saxon world.

Food Geography—Histories of a Forming Geographical Subdiscipline

This chapter outlines how the geographical study of food, its production and consumption, has evolved from a traditional agricultural geography, which focuses on structures and developments of agricultural economies and their spatially effective processes, to a food geography ('geography of food'). The 'geography of food' aims at the study of food systems (production, processing, transport, marketing, consumption). The starting point of the scientific study of agriculture—and in particular of the model explanation of agricultural land use—was marked by the Thünen Rings, which illustrate the relationship between land rent and agricultural production location and represent the latter as a sequence of concentric circles. This early model received a lot of attention in German-speaking, but also international geography in the 1960s and 1970s, and the regularities it formulated often served as a starting point for regional economic analyses (Robinson, 2004; Sick, 1983) In the early 1980s, the model itself was still credited with having "laid the foundations of agricultural geography that are still valid today" (Sick, 1983, p. 11). The importance of the model has been acknowledged up to the recent past. Heineberg (2003) comes to the conclusion that the approach is "unfortunately too simple to represent or explain complex socioeconomic structures" (Heineberg, 2003, p. 132) but appreciates the work as "one of the *essential* foundations for the development of spatial economics" (Heineberg, 2003, p. 131) and one that "still has a considerable didactic significance" (Heineberg, 2003, p. 132).

The classical or traditional agricultural geography, predominantly practiced in the first half of the twentieth century, (cf. Otremba, 1953; Troll, 1939) was more and more replaced in the German-speaking area by more social-geographically influenced works. Especially the researches of Bobek (1948) and Hartke (1956)which were characterized by a functional way of thinking and addressed social aggregates or social group-specific norms and values and their spatial effects, can be regarded as milestones of this development. From the 1960s

© The Author(s), under exclusive license to Springer Fachmedien Wiesbaden GmbH, part of Springer Nature 2022
T. Sedelmeier et al., *Foodscapes*, essentials,
https://doi.org/10.1007/978-3-658-36706-0_3

on, however, the first signs of a loss of importance of agricultural geography in the canon of geographic subdisciplines became apparent: Along with societal change and the associated processes such as urbanization, urban and population geographic issues as well as industrial geography as a subfield of economic geography gained in importance. Agricultural geography also took account of the changes and—against the background of the rapidly increasing importance of part-time farms compared to full-time farms, the growing industrial agricultural production as well as agrotourism—embedded its research focus more strongly in the geography of rural areas (Ruppert, 1984). Thus, already in the mid-1980s, Ruppert called for an "open" (Ruppert, 1984) agricultural geography, which should be dedicated to the issues of environmental protection, land management without agricultural production, resource provision function and multifunctional land use.

The international discourse on a new direction for agricultural geography also gains momentum during these years. In their groundbreaking article, Bowler and Ilbery (1987) call for a reorientation of agricultural geography, which should take place in three dimensions:

1. The conceptual orientation to the food supply system, accompanied by a shift in focus from the production of agricultural goods to their further processing, distribution and marketing.
2. Considering agricultural impacts on broader segments of society—both urban and rural.
3. Integrating perspectives and theories from political economy and agricultural sociology.

Atkins praises this attempt to reorient agricultural geography, but does not think it is broad enough: "Their revised agenda can be seen as state-of-the-artism rather than a true demolition and reconstruction job" (Atkins, 1988, p. 281). Instead, he argues for a transformation of agricultural geography into a 'geography of food' against the background of the declining economic value of agriculture in Great Britain and the growing importance of downstream processing and supply networks. He justifies this along three lines of argumentation: first, agraricultural geography has focused too much on agriculture in the Global North, leaving the Global South to development geography. While this has contributed to explaining exchange relations and the emergence of famines, it has neglected the study of food systems (production, processing, transportation, marketing, consumption). Second, he argues that little attention has been paid to the role of food—both unprocessed and processed—in the formation of global trade relations and the development of societies, nor has the capital investments of multinational corporations associated with food been systematically studied. Third, following the work of French geographers in the late 1970s, he suggests that consumer's dietary habits should be brought into the research focus, as food consumption and its social as well as economic consequences should not be ignored in the analysis of food supply systems. As an example, Atkins cites the relationship between diet and health and its spatial manifestations (Atkins, 1988). Agricultural geography is not capable of this, which is why it should be replaced by food geography: "Bowler and Ilbery have redefined agricultural geography in order to reproduce it. Let us be bolder. Agricultural geography is dead: long live the geography of food!" (Atkins, 1988, p. 282).

Atkins' claims are echoed and criticized in the German-speaking world by Bohle: "This swan song is premature and unnecessary" (Bohle, 1990, p. 23). He justifies this with reference to the work of Sick (cf. Sick, 1983), by arguing that conventional agricultural geography already contains all the substantive and theoretical approaches of the English discussion, and that a restriction to food geography would lead to a scientific "reduction in yield". (Bohle, 1990). Instead, Bohle and Krüger—drawing on the contributions of Bowler and Ilbery (1987) and Atkins (1988) propose a 'geography of food systems' that focuses on the "interface between food systems and economic and socio-political factors [...] in the study of hunger crises". (Bohle & Krüger, 1992, p. 258). It is therefore not surprising that, in the German-speaking world, food geography as a subfield of development geography focused in particular on access to food, food crises, and approaches to overcoming food insecurity in emerging economies and countries of the Global South (among many: Dittrich, 1995; Drescher, 1995; Krings, 1997; Lohnert, 1995; Tröger, 2004). Theoretically, many of these studies refer to the 'entitlement' and 'capability' approach Sens (among many: Sen, 1982, 1985) as well as Chambers' (1989) vulnerability approach. Moreover, in the Anglo-Saxon-speaking world, a new direction of food geography emerged: the 'geography of food consumption'. Although cultural geographers were studying food habits in various regions of North America and Britain as early as the 1960s, they often focused on supposed culinary curiosities. In the early 1980s and 1990s, the spectrum finally broadened to include studies that analyzed differences among states and population groups in consumption habits and their consequences (e.g., diet-related diseases of civilization), surveying subjects, food expenditures, and their quantities and weights (Grigg, 1995). These studies show that in Western industrialized countries a change in dietary habits already took place in the course of industrialization, which was characterized in particular by an increase in the consumption of meat, sugar, vegetables and fruit, while the proportion of starchy staple foods decreased. In countries of the Global South, on the other hand, this change took place with a considerable time lag and did not set in until the 1960s (Grigg, 1999).

Since the turn of the millennium, against the backdrop of a series of food scandals and advances in biotechnology for food production, which are viewed skeptically by the general public (especially in Europe), alternative food supply systems have gained prominence (Niles & Roff, 2008). Accordingly, the number of scientific publications addressing the regionality and seasonality of products, as well as their accessibility, has increased rapidly (among many: Goodman et al., 2011; Whatmore et al., 2003). These considerations have given rise to numerous studies that address issues of meal preparation, food rituals, special diets (e.g., veganism), and the relationship between food and identity, originating in anthropology (among many: Lévi-Strauss & Moldenhauer, 1976). This branch of food geography can be subsumed under the label 'critical food studies' (Colombino, 2014).The associated processes and actions of actors are in turn manifested in the so-called 'foodscapes' that will be addressed in the following chapter.

Recommended reading:

- Atkins (1988): an article still worth reading that was instrumental in the development of food geography.
- Robinson (2004): A very good overview of the historical development and current agricultural and food geography issues.
- Ruppert (1984): A very readable overview of the development of German-language agricultural geography.

The Multidimensionality of the Concept of 'foodscapes'

4

The term 'foodscape' first found its way into the scientific literature in the mid-1990s (Yasmeen, 1996) and was only very hesitantly taken up by other authors in the following years. It was not until 2010 that the number of scientific publications using the term increased noticeably. Vonthron et al. (2020) identify four different approaches to 'foodsapes' underlying the corresponding studies:

1. Spatial approaches that use quantitative data and statistical methods to measure the impact of 'foodscapes' on residents' diets and health.
2. Social and cultural science approaches that analyze structural inequalities based on quantitative surveys and qualitative interviews.
3. Behavioral approaches that examine at the level of individuals how their perceptions influence their eating behaviors.
4. Systemic approaches that unite critique of the global food regime and promotion of regional as well as sustainable diets.

Although there are a growing number of studies internationally—especially in North America, but also in Great Britain and Scandinavia—that draw on 'foodscapes' as a conceptual framing, in the German-speaking world, with few exceptions, (Sedelmeier, 2018, 2019; Sperk & Kistemann, 2012) there are hardly any studies in the German-speaking world that refer to the term 'foodscape' or its German-language counterpart "Nahrungslandschaft".

As is not uncommon with social science terms, the term itself is defined and conceptualized in a variety of ways. Common to all attempts at definition is that, on the one hand, they understand 'foodscapes' as physical-material manifestations whose design is shaped by the actions of actors and charged with subjective interpretations (Sedelmeier, 2018). A widely cited definition that focuses on meaning and attributions is offered by MacKendrick: "Consider the spaces and

© The Author(s), under exclusive license to Springer Fachmedien Wiesbaden Gmbh, part of Springer Nature 2022
T. Sedelmeier et al., *Foodscapes*, essentials,
https://doi.org/10.1007/978-3-658-36706-0_4

places where you acquire food, prepare food, talk about food and gather some sort of meaning from food. This is your foodscape" (MacKendrick, 2014). This definition shows that the foodscape—as it was a requirement of Atkins (see Chap. 3)—includes the entire chain from production to consumption and also includes all actions and actors that influence the processes or are influenced by these processes. Adema (2006, p. 12) refers to 'foodscapes' as "an Emulsion of Food and Landscape" and points out that these become visible and effective on different scales: for example, in the actions of multinational food corporations, the associated global exchange, which in turn fosters the spread of (post)modern food practices; but also on a local and individual level, when it comes to procurement channels, forms of preparation, as well as the incorporation of food and associated effects (e.g. health) on human bodies (Adema, 2006). In summary, it can be stated that foodscapes are shaped by socio-cultural, economic and political as well as physical influences on the macro- and micro-level (Lake, 2018; MacKendrick, 2014) and these set the 'stage' (structure in the sense of the structuration theory according to Giddens 1984) for the actions of actors and that these two (action and structure) mutually influence each other (Clary et al., 2017).

Due to the openness and multiperspectivity of the concept, its use as an analytical framework in empirical studies requires some stipulations: 'Foodscapes' contain quantifiable as well as mappable elements, but a limitation to those is not reasonable! Instead, following the understanding of the social construction of foodscapes, a methodological approach to the subject must always be based on qualitative research methods (e.g. narrative interviews, ero-epic conversations). A methodological triangulation seems to be the most promising approach. Nevertheless, the study by Vonthron et al. (2020) which evaluated a total of 140 articles with reference to 'foodscapes' and analyzed them with regard to definitions and contexts of use, makes clear that, especially in spatial studies, mainly statistical procedures and geographic information systems are chosen as methodological approaches. In addition, the understanding of foodscapes is essentially limited to the occurrence of food offerings in the form of restaurants, snack bars, etc. in a neighborhood. Some of these studies also provide an analysis based on the spatial distribution of food offerings as to how this affects parts of life that are considered central. This includes, for example, questions about the relationship between food supply in a neighborhood and the socioeconomic status of its residents and the impact of the supply structure on dietary behavior (Vonthron et al., 2020). Perception-based studies, on the other hand, ask how a person's perception of the food landscape affects their dietary behavior. In systemic approaches, critical perspectives on the global food system predominate and alternative production and distribution systems are sought (Vonthron et al., 2020).

The perspectives on 'foodscapes' listed above illustrate that access to them is a crucial criterion. Access can be broken down into a number of areas: 'availability' refers to the presence of a food offer that meets one's taste preferences and nutritional needs; 'accessibility' refers to the distance between the offer location and a person's residence; 'affordability' includes the level of food prices in relation to the customers' financial margins; 'accommodation' and 'acceptability' refer to store opening hours and availability of parking facilities as well as to the shopping ambience (Clary et al., 2017). Evidently, the access to foodscapes is not only manifold but also very individual. Their concrete use depends on a person's predispositions, their endowment with social, economic and symbolic capital as well as time resources. Time restrictions, for example, due to long working hours or insufficient childcare facilities for small children, can lead to a significant limitation of the action space and to the fact that only grocery stores are visited that can be combined with other activities (Clary et al., 2017). In addition, it can be observed that the foodscape of economically better-off milieus—whether for reasons of time or convenience—is increasingly expanding into virtual spaces, by an increasing usage of delivery services of supermarket chains (MacKendrick, 2014). A lack of financial resources, on the other hand, can lead to the purchase of fresh, healthy food being neglected in favor of other needs, or to food shopping being limited to a few, particularly low-priced suppliers (e.g. discounters; (Clary et al., 2017). A not inconsiderable proportion of households in countries of the Global North are also dependent on food donations from charitable institutions (see Sect. 6.1; MacKendrick, 2014). This does appear to be problematic, since there are numerous studies, both for the German-speaking countries and at the international level, which highlight the fact that the use of such assistance is shame-ridden. Moreover, it shows that groups of people are excluded from this assistance on the basis of specific characteristics (e.g. addictive behavior, mental illness) and that the relevant institutions are—unintentionally—involved in the substitution of basic welfare state rights by a system of charity (among many: Miewald & McCann, 2014; Sedelmeier, 2013; Selke, 2009; Wakefield et al., 2012; Warshawsky, 2010). The number of scientific publications that come to a more positive assessment of such food aid is much smaller. Reference should be made here to a recent study which, using the example of so-called 'social groceries' in Belgium, comes to the conclusion that assistance can be provided with respect for human dignity and recognition of the status as a customer if three basic conditions are met: "product choice, the act of paying, and recognition of the need for appropriate food" (Andriessen et al., 2020, p. 15).

At this point, a short interim conclusion should be made: We were able to establish that the 'foodscapes' can serve as a framework for diverse questions related to the production, consumption and symbolic charging of food. In particular, publications that address social disparities and health issues in the context of diets predominate. In short: Foodscapes are problematized! In this context, foodscapes are often conceptually specified as so-called 'food deserts' or—more rarely—'food swamps'. Therefore, we want to deal with these terms and the understandings behind them in the following.

Both terms originate from the debate around problematic food situations of urban households in precarious living situations in countries of the Global North (especially the UK, Canada, and the US), with 'food deserts' being the more widely used and substantively broader term, and 'food swamps' can be considered as "a companion metaphor to food deserts" (Elton, 2019, p. 371) Swamps have long been considered disease-ridden places, where disease is transmitted by swarms of mosquitoes, and danger from scary creatures lurking in the murky water-whether imaginary or real, such as alligators-was ubiquitous (Elton, 2019). The apparent danger posed by these places has been metaphorically applied by health researchers to urban spaces-often low-income neighborhoods-where there is a concentration of food establishments whose offerings are associated with unhealthy diets, such as fast-food restaurants (Minaker, 2016). This also allows the term 'food swamp' to be differentiated from another term that has been widely spread, particularly in medical studies, but also in social science publications: that of the 'obesogenic environment' (among many: Bagwell, 2011; Burgoine et al., 2011; Colls & Evans, 2014; Guthman, 2013; Lake et al., 2010). This encompasses biological and other environmental influences as well as other factors that influence behavior (e.g., advertising), whereas 'food swamps' refers explicitly to the structure of food supply in an area. The latter are not uncontroversial as a metaphor, as the negative connotations to swamps are only partly true, since *essential* as places of high biodiversity they take on an important ecological function, contribute to natural clarification of water, and also provide an important reservoir to balance flood tides (Elton, 2019).

Thus, while in the concept of 'food swamps' the danger is seen as essentially conditioned by the high incidence of fast-food restaurants, the term 'food desert' rather suggests a shortage. In fact, these 'food deserts' are understood as (urban) places where there is no or only very limited access to healthy food for the inhabitants (Shaw, 2006). Barriers to access can exist in many areas but are mainly addressed in economic (lack of financial capital in a household) as well as physical (limited mobility of individuals) terms. In empirical studies, access to healthy food was (and is) often equated with access to supermarkets (Cummins et al., 2008; Cummins & Macintyre, 1999). This can be justified by the fact that supermarkets, as full-line retailers, stock foods that are generally considered healthy, such as fresh, unprocessed fruits and vegetables. However, focusing on access to supermarkets seems problematic because it excludes a variety of sources of fresh food, such as greengrocers and local weekly markets (Shannon, 2014). Equally debatable is the attribution of a food as healthy or unhealthy, as a healthy diet is composed of a variety of foods with very different characteristics. In empirical studies, foods that are low in energy density are often operationalized as healthy, while those that are very high in fat and sugar are considered unhealthy (Wright et al., 2016).

Since access also depends on accessibility, spatial distances often form a central criterion and thresholds are set, for example for 'walking distances' that are considered reasonable (Morton & Blanchard, 2007). However, these generalized standardizations can be viewed critically, as physical conditions are distributed very differently across different population groups (Wright et al., 2016). What is still a walking distance for an athletic young woman can be an insurmountable distance for an obese senior citizen. This already shows that the positivist understanding of 'food desert' as "a physical object that is independent of observation and can be captured and described by empirical methods" (at least in the U.S., e.g. Michelle Obama's Let's Move campaign; Kühne, 2013, p. 130) must be complemented by a social constructivist perspective that regards 'food deserts' not as objectively measurable spatial manifestations, but as a relationality that is first constructed through the relationships or interactions of acting actors (Sedelmeier, 2019). Following and complementing Shaw's classification of food deserts, who supplemented the common access barriers 'ability' (physical skills) and 'asset' (financial means) by the factor of individual attitudes, e.g. in the form of food taboos, these three dimensions are to be extended by the factor of 'attitude' (Shaw, 2006). These three dimensions are to be extended by the factor of social capital, since this makes it possible to compensate for deficits in the other three areas (Sedelmeier, 2019).

Recommended reading:

- Elton (2019): This critical examination of the notion of 'food swamps' is highly interesting.
- Shaw (2006): The paper is still relevant and represents the first attempt to classify 'food deserts'.
- Vonthron et al. (2020): For those interested in learning more about the different branches of research within 'foodscapes', this is a good initial overview.

The Impact of Political or Social Systems on 'foodscapes'

5

The expression of 'foodscapes' is strongly dependent on societal frameworks. These in turn are strongly linked to the ideological/political character of society. The impact of different political or social systems on material spaces has been discussed in numerous publications (for instance at: Kirchhoff, 2019; Kirchhoff & Trepl, 2001; Kühne, 2011, 2015; Kühne et al., 2015; Vicenzotti, 2011), insofar we will briefly present the results in the following—focused on 'foodscapes'. In doing so, we follow the order of historical appearance of the political idea systems and start with considerations on the liberal state, then present *essential* aspects of a socialist society, and then lead over to the welfare state as it is characteristic for Western European societies, which can be understood as situated between the poles of the liberal and the socialist society (for instance: Fassmann 2009).

Essential tenets of liberalism lie in the following axioms: that man is born free, endowed with equal rights, inherently good, and endowed with reason. Politically, liberalism calls for the "defense of certain individual rights and freedoms, such as freedom of expression, refraining from discrimination on the basis of race, sex, or nationality, procedural rights (e.g., the right of defense), and political rights to democratic participation and involvement in elections" (Rivera López 1995, p. 17). For him, the market economy as a form of economy is derived from these fundamental considerations, as it is the only form of economic activity "which is in harmony with the individual fundamental right of freedom and offers the best framework conditions for a self-responsible organization of life" (Kersting, 2009, p. 29). If this is understood as a social framework, it entails consequences in dealing with spaces and not least on foodscapes: the strong orientation of food on criteria of economic efficiency affects production, transport and distribution. In production this means a rational agriculture in large units (large plots in land management, mass animal husbandry, etc.; see also: Ipsen, 2006), in transport a preference of the transport system with low costs (from pick-up truck over

T. Sedelmeier et al., *Foodscapes*, essentials,
https://doi.org/10.1007/978-3-658-36706-0_5

railroad to airplane or container ship) and in distribution an assortment, which is demanded with the clientele. This assortment can differ greatly as a result of the strong economic and (related) milieu-specific clientele, which is particularly evident in the United States with its distinctive free-market orientation (see case study in Sect. 6.2). Since not least poverty and reduced access to healthy food and education are associated with the restriction of basic rights, liberals who place individual life chances at the center of their considerations see the tasks of the state as broader than in the establishment of a reliable legal framework and the guarantee of internal and external security (cf: Dahrendorf, 1979; Rawls, 1993).

Socialists see the equality rights formulated by liberalism as incomplete, since they extended to political participation alone, not to economic participation (Marx, 2014 [1872]). Accordingly, the expropriation and socialization of the means of production are seen as prerequisites for an egalitarian society. In terms of 'foodscapes', this is associated with a human entitlement to access to 'healthy food', regardless of where one lives (socio-economic status does not matter in an egalitarian society). Efforts to implement socialist ideas, however, produced results with 'real socialism' that showed a divergence from the ideals: The expropriation of means of production usually involved the killing, expulsion, or at least internal emigration of the former owners, which entailed a loss of specific knowledge of the technical, organizational, and economic control of means of production. This was associated with a loss of efficiency that was often greater than the gains for those who were to benefit from the expropriations. Their disappointment was responded to with reprisals, which, made the economy more inefficient. The resulting 'economy of scarcity' (Kornai, 1980) had—in conjunction with efforts to 'urbanize rural life' to create more egalitarian living conditions (and the model could only be the city as the seat of labor, normatively the engine of socialism)—significant effects on 'foodscapes': The physical spaces of production were aligned with the conditions of mass production, transportation was via congested transport routes, and distribution was via centrally controlled units. This, in combination with the widespread absenteeism of the workforces at all levels of production and organization, led to a loss-making focus on the production and distribution of cheap food. The production of healthy food was thus handed over (contrary to the very idea of socialism) to private initiative in home gardens or weekend housing complexes. Extensive central state influence would have made a different organization of space possible, but not least the bureaucratic effort, the preference for production over distribution (which meant in particular a delayed supply of newly built quarters also with goods for daily needs), the degree of administration of production facilities, the low potential for innovation, etc. in real socialism reduced the supply of all parts of society with healthy (and without major ecological damage) produced food (among many: Czepczyński, 2008; Degórska, 2007; Domański, 1997; Kornai, 1992; Kühne, 2002, 2003; Kühne et al., 2015; Smith, 1996).

The welfare state idea can be characterized as an effort to minimize the unintended side effects of implementing (economic) liberal and socialist ideals. This concerns, on the one hand, the tendencies of polarization producing inequalities of opportunity in a social order following a classical liberal ideal, and, on the other hand, the economic inefficiencies of the real socialist social system (along with its political repressions). Welfare states pursue this goal of minimizing the respective unintended side effects by guaranteeing political liberties and economic state transfers. This is of importance for the topic 'foodscapes', since state interventions in the rights of disposal of private land use exist (Rothstein, 2001; Scharpf, 1998 [1996]). Thus, the welfare state reserves the right to regulate the type and extent of use of an area (e.g. whether a parcel of land is dedicated to residential development, commercial or agricultural activity, etc.; it is also possible to regulate through planning how high the proportion of built-up area is, how many stories buildings may have, etc.),.It intervenes both in terms of regulatory law (e.g. through the Building Use Ordinance or the Neighborhood Law)in the concrete use and design of areas and through subsidy law (e.g. in agriculture) in the intensity of use. In the transport of food (and not only food), considerations are taken into account to minimize side effects (e.g. of an ecological nature). The same applies to the control of retail trade through the designation of areas for this use, whereby the range of products is again left to entrepreneurial calculation (as is the calculation of whether a store can be operated profitably on the designated area; see also Chilla et al., 2016; Heinritz et al., 2003; Kulke, 2001; Langhagen-Rohrbach, 2010).

Recommended reading:

- Domański (1997): Comprehensive insight into the logics of real socialist spatial design, with a focus on urban developments.
- Kirchhoff (2019): Sound yet concise overview of the context of political ideas in relation to landscape.
- Langhagen-Rohrbach (2010): Insight into the possibilities and limits of the state-administrative ordering of spaces, using the example of the Federal Republic of Germany.

'Poverty Foodscapes'—Two Case Studies

6

The case studies presented in the following refer to a welfare state (Germany) and a state with a strong market economy (United States) in order to provide a more in-depth look at current developments in foodscapes. Since foodscapes of real socialist states today are rather historical recordings, we have refrained from including such a case study.

In the second case study, we also show, using the example of Baton Rouge, Louisiana, how a theoretical and methodological broadening of 'foodscapes' research can be carried out.

6.1 The Tafel food bank

As shown in Chap. 4, access to 'foodscapes' depends on several dimensions, including affordability, which is the interaction between the prices of the food supply and a person's or household's endowment of financial capital (Clary et al., 2017). Despite relatively low food prices—compared to the rest of Europe—and a comparatively efficient welfare state, a growing number of people in Germany are forced to save on food costs due to rising living costs in other areas (Sedelmeier, 2011). Since the mid-1990s, food banks have been filling these gaps. Against this background, the question arises whether these facilities can meaningfully supplement the foodscapes of socially worse off people and thus contribute to overcoming precarious living situations.

The first Tafel was founded in Berlin in 1993, modeled on Feeding America, a U.S. nonprofit organization that collects unsaleable food from supermarkets and gives it to the needy (Grell, 2010). Until the end of 2004, the Berliner Tafel operated purely as a food bank: it supplied women's shelters, homeless shelters, and other social institutions, but did not have its own distribution points or food banks. Only since 2005 has it been operating distribution points in cooperation with church congregations in the Berlin metropolitan area (Sedelmeier, 2011). Most food banks in Germany operate their own distribution points where users can obtain food after providing proof of need (usually receipt of basic social security benefits, such as unemployment benefit II in Germany). The food is distributed for a small fee, the so-called symbolic coin (usually one or two euros), but there are also—mainly in southern Germany—food banks that price the food individually and sell it to users for a price of 10–20% of the original store price (Sedelmeier, 2011, 2018). When we speak of users and not of customers here, we do so deliberately: customers "appear equipped with purchasing power, are sovereign, and choose the offer and the provider. But all this does not apply to the Tafel customers, because they cannot select, but must take what the abundance society has left" (Segbers, 2011, p. 480).

The range of goods offered by the food banks consists mainly of food that has a limited shelf life and is usually close to or past its best-before date, but is still fit for consumption, and fresh food, such as unprocessed fruit and vegetables, which food retailers no longer sell to their customers and donate to the food bank. Goods that can be kept for a longer period of time, so-called 'dry food' such as coffee and pasta, are hardly represented in the assortment (Sedelmeier, 2011). In addition to food, some food banks now also offer products from the non-food segment as well as non-material offers, such as cooking courses. The latter, however, "can also be perceived by the food bank users as paternalistic encroachment" (Wolff, 2016, p. 7). The food banks are operated either by sponsors (e.g. Caritas, Diakonie) or in the form of registered associations. The common umbrella organization of the food banks is Tafel Deutschland e.V., founded in 1995, which monitors compliance with the food bank principles, supports the food banks in their operations and represents their interests at national level (e.g., vis-à-vis politicians; Sedelmeier, 2011, 2018). Especially, the socio-political lobbying, however, is often criticized (among many: Sedelmeier, 2011; Selke, 2009), since it is perceived as insufficient: "This socio-political work has been neglected by the 'Tafelbewegung' so far. Tafel have allowed themselves to be instrumentalized all too naively and have thereby enabled socio-political regressions for the people" (Bruckdorfer, 2013, p. 21).

Lack of political commitment is not the only criticism addressed at the food banks; instead, there are a multitude of reasons why the food banks do not enrich the foodscapes of people in need. Some of the arguments will be presented below. Despite the large number of Tafeln, currently about 950 in Germany (as of July 2021), there are clear regional priorities in the distribution. In rural areas, as well as in the northeast overall, the Tafel density is significantly lower than in the south of Germany, despite the fact that the usual indicators of prosperity (average household income, assets, etc.) are lower and the usual indicators of poverty (e.g., poverty risk ratio) are higher in the'new' German states. This suggests that the prevalence of Tafeln does not correlate with the occurrence of poverty—in fact, the opposite is true (Sedelmeier, 2013). In addition to spatial distribution, supply also plays a crucial role. The per capita amount of food per food bank user has been decreasing over the years (Normann, 2009). This means that the already very fluctuating supply is becoming less attractive due to the quantitative decline. At the same time, for a significant proportion of users, visiting the food banks is accompanied by embarrassment and stigmatization (among many: Molling, 2009; Sedelmeier, 2011; Selke, 2009; *La polyphonie linguistique* 2009; Selke, 2014), which is also due—in addition to the public queuing—to the fact that reciprocity is suspended, since the users accept the food "without being able to provide an adequate service in return at the same time" (Maar, 2010, p. 236). This is all the more serious because, with the establishment of the food banks, a system has developed that threatens to replace welfare state rights (and thus poverty reduction) piece by piece with poor relief (and thus poverty alleviation; among many: Molling, 2009; Segbers, 2011; Selke, 2009).

6.2   Baton Rouge—Plank Road, from historical and spatial contextualization of a 'poverty foodscape' to its phenomenological experience

Louisiana's capital, Baton Rouge, with a population of about 230 thousand, is among the most fragmented metropolitan areas in the United States in terms of ethnicity, voting patterns, and socioeconomic status (Dottle, 2019; Kühne & Jenal, 2020a). In particular, in a space of nearly triangular layout bounded by Florida Boulevard, Airline Highway, and Interstate 110, live predominantly people of African American descent who face low household incomes, a high risk of poverty, high crime rates, at the same time a worn out (even by the standards of the rest of Baton Rouge) technical infrastructure (which will be addressed later), reduced access to higher education—and to healthy food (Figs. 6.1 and 6.2). Due

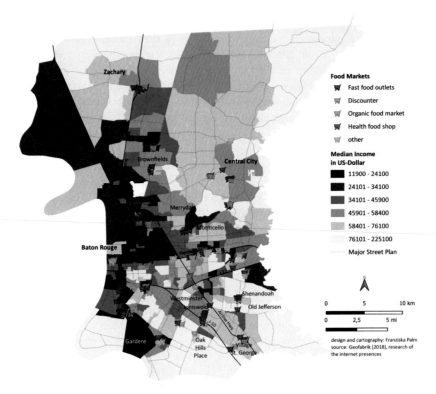

Fig. 6.1 The distribution of grocery stores in Baton Rouge in 2021 (Map: Franziska Palm (2021, in press), with kind reprint permission)

to these living conditions, Kühne and Jenal (2021) characterize, referring to Ralf Dahrendorf's (1979), this concept of life chances as a 'triangle of reduced life chances'. Here culminate global, national, regional, but also Baton Rouge-specific local developments, which have been discussed in more detail elsewhere (Kühne et al., 2020; Kühne & Jenal, 2020a, 2020b, 2020c, 2021). The global trend of segregation is reinforced in Baton Rouge by an ethnic polarization that has been strong in the southern United States since the end of slavery.The traditionally low tendency of administrative penetration of society in Louisiana culminates in Baton Rouge in a historically developed, far-reaching abstinence from spatial planning (see already Bartholomew 1945–1948; Brill 1963). In the context of the oil price crisis of the 1980s (low oil prices), the great dependence of Louisiana's

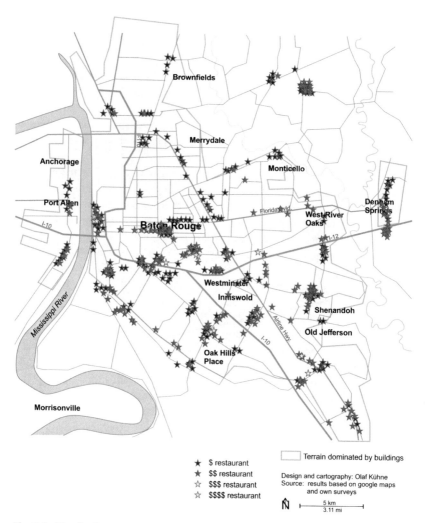

Fig. 6.2 The distribution of restaurants in Baton Rouge and their price allocation according to google maps. (slightly modified from: Kühne & Jenal, 2020a)

(and Baton Rouge's) economy on the petrochemical industry led to the loss of well-paying jobs for people with low skills; in Baton Rouge, this particularly affected the African American population east of Interstate 110 (west of which is the Exxon refinery). The (African American) population north of Florida Boulevard did not benefit, or benefited only indirectly, from the development of and around Louisiana State University (LSU, located south of the city): Students, faculty, and administrative staff are of non-African American origin (mostly white), and their residences cluster around the university (also as a result of congested roads), leading not least to the gentrification of neighborhoods with dominant African American populations (and their displacement).

If the supply of (healthy) food is not oriented towards the increase of life chances but towards criteria of economic efficiency, a situation arises as it can be found in Baton Rouge: the few grocery stores carry an assortment that offers high-caloric food at a low price. A supermarket visited during a 'phenomenological walk' (by Corinna Jenal and Olaf Kühne) along Plank Road, which crosses the 'triangle of reduced life chances', made this development physically experienceable: Bulk containers of ready-made burgers and French Fries, cheap sweet drinks in large-volume containers dominated the food offer, flanked by partly empty shelves, in which—if available—a basic offer for basic needs was presented (cleaning agents, garbage bags, buckets, some tools of low price and just as low quality). The supermarket gave the impression that the building and the interior had hardly been renovated since it was built (1960s architecture). The staff's interaction with (the few customers) was characterized by a spirited gruffness. This supermarket was also the only one on Plank Road, a thriving shopping street before the oil crisis. Partially destroyed light signs, faded store signs above boarded-up windows, parking spaces in front of closed stores (free of cars ready for operation) still bear witness to those times. The few economic activities are largely limited to the sale of alcohol (liquor stores), cheap instant meals. Additionally several (especially through bars in front of the windows) pawn shops can be found. Bullet holes in buildings document that private security along Plank Road is of existential importance. Garbage (often packaging of the high-calorie foods mentioned at the beginning) and other refuse (up to a largely decomposed carcass of a dog in the street gutter) are visually, sometimes olfactorily present. The sidewalks along Plank Road—where present—are in a condition that presents a high potential for danger to life and limb of pedestrians, particularly in the form of (unsecured) potholes, often several decimeters deep. The number of people walking is (accordingly?) low. Acoustically, car traffic dominates, especially – temporarily—strongly tuned youngtimer limousines with barely muffled exhaust systems and audio systems (mostly fed with Baton Rouge rap) compete for acoustic presence. These impressions are strangely contradictory to the overall calm, peaceful and friendly atmosphere, which spans between the researchers (white skin color) and the place and the people staying here (African-American origin).

Conclusion

7

The topic of 'foodscapes' has only been the subject of scientific investigation for about two and a half decades and has since emerged as a thriving field of research with well over one hundred peer reviewed publications (Vonthron et al., 2020). This *Essential* provided a theoretical and thematic overview in this regard. The latter showed the diversity of issues, ofproduction, distribution and consumption of food, the problem of limited access to food, but also the dependence of the expression of 'foodscapes' on social systems (or political systems).

The theoretical overview included the 'scape' perspective, i.e. syntheses of material objects in relational arrangement on the one hand, social construction processes on the other. This allows recourse to theories (but also methods) of landscape research, whose tradition goes back far more than two centuries. While this comparatively recent history of 'foodscapes' research relieves it, on the one hand, of the conflicts surrounding the paradigm shift in the course of (largely) replacing the essentialist approach, on the other hand, there is also still a great potential forusing currently discussed different theoretical perspectives on the topic. Thus, in the research on 'foodscapes' to date, positivist framings in partic-ular, and in parts also social constructivist framings, dominate. The potentials of the other theoretical perspectives of current landscape research have hardly been exploited so far. the case study of Baton Rouge in this '*Essential*', in which, among other things, a phenomenological approach to 'foodscapes' was chosen, shows that this is indeed possible. Research from a discourse-theoretical perspec-tive (for example, on the discursive actualization of the topic in social media) is just as pending as a radical constructivist-systems-theoretical approach (for exam-ple, on the resonance of the topic in different social subsystems). The same also applies, for example, to the experience of 'food deserts' by those affected and

T. Sedelmeier et al., *Foodscapes*, essentials,
https://doi.org/10.1007/978-3-658-36706-0_7

their attribution of meaning to material objects from the perspective of assemblage theory. Also, the focus on interconnectedness in 'foodscapes' could be a relevant use case for ANT.

In this respect, the synthesis of the current state of 'foodscapes' research still remains in a state that can be described as 'incomplete-neopragmatic'. This leads us to Karl Popper's spotlight metaphor (Popper, 2003[1945]). This metaphor compares scientific theories with spotlights, which illuminate a research object from different directions. Complex objects require a multitude of theories (spotlights) in order to illuminate the different aspects of the object. The topic 'foodscapes' is very complex due to its variety of spatial, social, political, economic and cultural aspects. In this respect, the application of only a few theoretical perspectives leaves numerous aspects of the complex subject 'foodscapes' still unexplored. This results in a great potential for future research on the subject complex.

What You Learned From This *essential*

- The scientific study of foodscapes is gaining importance not only in the study of food systems with questions of production, processing, transport, marketing of food, but also in the discussion of topics such as urban health, life chances, vulnerability, and many more.
- Already in the comparatively young history of the sub-discipline, a certain multidimensionality of the concept of foodscapes has emerged, which can be divided into different approaches (spatial, socio-cultural, behavioral, systemic), but whose potential with regard to theoretical as well as methodological approaches, from the authors' point of view, has hardly been exploited so far in view of its increasing importance.
- This *Essential* points to possible further perspectives on foodscapes-related research and encourages discussion of its expansion

T. Sedelmeier et al., *Foodscapes*, essentials,
https://doi.org/10.1007/978-3-658-36706-0

References

Aas, Ø., Qvenild, M., Wold, L. C., Jacobsen, G. B., & Ruud, A. (2017). Local opposition against high-voltage grids: public responses to agency-caused science-policy trolls. *Journal of Environmental Policy & Planning, 19* (4), 347–359. https://doi.org/10.1080/152 3908X.2016.1213625.

Adema, P. (2006). *Festive Foodscapes: Iconizing food and the shaping of identity and place.* University of Texas Press.

Adema, P. (2010). *Garlic capital of the World. Gilroy, garlic, and the making of a festive foodscape.* University Press of Mississippi.

Alban, E., Wolf, K., & Hauzar, D. (2000). *Regionalatlas Rhein-Main. Natur – Gesellschaft – Wirtschaft (Veröffentlichungen der Gesellschaft für Regionalwissenschaftliche Forschung Rhein-Main* (Regio Rhein-Main) e. V, vol. 15). Selbstverlag "Rhein-Mainische Forschung".

Albert, G. (2005). *Hermeneutischer Positivismus und dialektischer Essentialismus Vilfredo Paretos.* VS Verlag.

Allen, C. D. (2011). On actor-network theory and landscape. *Area, 43* (3), 274–280. https://doi.org/10.1111/j.1475-4762.2011.01026.x.

Andriessen, T., van der Horst, H., & Morrow, O. (2020). "Consumer is king": Staging consumer culture in a food aid organization. *Journal of Consumer Culture,* (1–20). https://doi.org/10.1177/1469540520935950.

Antrop, M. (2019). A brief history of landscape research. In P. Howard, I. Thompson, E. Waterton, & M. Atha (Eds.), *The routledge companion to landscape studies* (2nd ed., pp. 1–16). Routledge.

Atkins, P. J. (1988). Redefining agricultural geography as the geography of food. *Area, 20* (3), 281–283.

Bagwell, S. (2011). The role of independent fast-food outlets in obesogenic environments: A case study of east London in the UK. *Environment and Planning A: Economy and Space,43*(9), 2217–2236. https://doi.org/10.1068/a44110.

Bartholomew, H. (1945–1948). *The 25 Year-Parish Plan for Metropolitan Baton Rouge.Louisiana.* Eigenverlag.

Berr, K., & Kühne, O. (2020). „*Und das ungeheure Bild der Landschaft …". The Genesis of Landscape Understanding in the German-speaking Regions.* Springer VS.

Berr, K., & Schenk, W. (2019). Begriffsgeschichte. In O. Kühne, F. Weber, K. Berr, & C. Jenal (Eds.), *Handbuch Landschaft* (pp. 23–38). Springer VS.

Bobek, H. (1948). Stellung und Bedeutung der Sozialgeographie. *Erdkunde, 2*(1/3), 118–125.

Bohle, H.-G. (1990). Von der Agrargeographie zur Nahrungsgeographie? Anmerkungen zu einer englischen Diskussion, mit Beispielen aus Indien. In B. Mohr, K. Sonntag, & J. Stadelbauer (Eds.), *Räumliche Strukturen im Wandel. Festschrift für W.D. Sick. Teil B: Beiträge zur Agrarwirtschaft der Tropen* (Freiburger Geographische Hefte, vol. 30, pp. 11–25). Selbstverlag der Universität Freiburg.

Bohle, H.-G., & Krüger, F. (1992). Perspektiven geographischer Nahrungskrisenforschung. *Die Erde – Journal of the Geographical Society of Berlin, 123*(4), 257–266.

Bourassa, S. C. (1991). *The aesthetics of landscape.* Belhaven Press.

Bowler, I. R., & Ilbery, B. W. (1987). Redefining agricultural geography. *Area, 19*(4), 327–332.

Brill, D. (1963). *Baton Rouge, LA. Aufstieg, Funktionen und Gestalt einer jungen Großstadt des neuen Industriegebietes am unteren Mississippi* (Schriften des Geographischen Instituts der Universität Kiel, vol. 21,2). Selbstverlag des Geographischen Instituts der Universität Kiel.

Bruckdorfer, M. (2013). Das Verhältnis von Sozialer Arbeit und „Tafeln". Die Position der Diakonie Deutschland. *Sozial Extra: Zeitschrift für soziale Arbeit,37*(5/6), 21–24. https://doi.org/10.1007/s12054-013-1011-4.

Burgoine, T., Alvanides, S., & Lake, A. A. (2011). Assessing the obesogenic environment of North East England. *Health and Place, 17*(3), 738–747. https://doi.org/10.1016/j.health place.2011.01.011.

Büttner, N. (2006). *Geschichte der Landschaftsmalerei.* Hirmer.

Chambers, R. (1989). Vulnerability, coping and policy. *IDS-Bulletin, 20*(2), 1–7.

Chilla, T., Kühne, O., Weber, F., & Weber, F. (2015). „Neopragmatische" Argumente zur Vereinbarkeit von konzeptioneller Diskussion und Praxis der Regionalentwicklung. In O. Kühne & F. Weber (Eds.), *Bausteine der Regionalentwicklung* (pp. 13–24). Springer VS.

Chilla, T., Kühne, O., & Neufeld, M. (2016). *Regionalentwicklung* (UTB, vol. 4566). Ulmer.

Clary, C., Matthews, S. A., & Kestens, Y. (2017). Between exposure, access and use: Reconsidering foodscape influence on dietary behaviour. *Health and Place, 44* (1–7). https://doi.org/10.1016/j.healthplace.2016.12.005.

Colls, R., & Evans, B. (2014). Making space for fat bodies? *Progress in Human Geography, 38*(6), 733–753. https://doi.org/10.1177/0309132513500373.

Colombino, A. (2014). The geography of food. *Bollettino della Società Geografica Italiana, 7*(13), 647–656.

Cosgrove, D. (1984). *Social formation and symbolic landscape.* University of Wisconsin Press.

Cummins, S., & Macintyre, S. (1999). The location of food stores in urban areas: a case study in Glasgow. *British Food Journal, 101*(7), 545–553. https://doi.org/10.1108/000707099 10279027.

Cummins, S., Findlay, A., Higgins, C., Petticrew, M., Sparks, L., & Thomson, H. (2008). Reducing inequalities in health and diet: Findings from a study on the impact of a food retail development. *Environment and Planning A: Economy and Space, 40*(2), 402–422. https://doi.org/10.1068/a38371.

Czepczyński, M. (2008). *Cultural landscapes of post-socialist cities. Representation of powers and needs.* Ashgate.

Dahrendorf, R. (1979). *Lebenschancen. Anläufe zur sozialen und politischen Theorie* (Suhrkamp-Taschenbuch, vol. 559). Suhrkamp.

Degórska, B. (2007). Key problems in the relation between the environment and spatial development in Poland. *European Spatial Research and Policy, 14*(2), 53–81.

Denevan, W. M., & Mathewson, K. (Eds.). (2009). *Carl sauer on culture and landscape. Readings and commentaries.* Louisiana State University Press.

Dittrich, C. (1995). *Ernährungssicherung und Entwicklung in Nordpakistan. Nahrungskrisen und Verwundbarkeit im peripheren Hochgebirgsraum* (Freiburger Studien zur geographischen Entwicklungsforschung, vol. 11). Verlag für Entwicklungspolitik (Zugl.: Freiburg (Breisgau), Univ., Diss., 1994).

Domański, B. (1997). *Industrial control over the socialist town: Benevolence or exploitation?* Praeger Publishers.

Dottle, R. (FiveThirtyEight, Ed.). (2019). Where democrats and republicans live in your city. Republicans and democrats tend not to live side-by-side, even when they live in the same city. https://projects.fivethirtyeight.com/republicans-democrats-cities/. Accessed: 13 Dec 2019.

Drescher, A. W. (1995). Traditionelle und rezente Landnutzung und Ernährungssicherung im Sambestial (Gwembe-Distrikt/Südsambia). *Petermanns Geographische Mitteilungen, 139*(5–6), 305–322.

Drexler, D. (2013). Die Wahrnehmung der Landschaft – ein Blick auf das englische, französische und ungarische Landschaftsverständnis. In D. Bruns & O. Kühne (Eds.), *Landschaften: Theorie, Praxis und internationale Bezüge. Impulse zum Landschaftsbegriff mit seinen ästhetischen, ökonomischen, sozialen und philosophischen Bezügen mit dem Ziel, die Verbindung von Theorie und Planungspraxis zu stärken* (pp. 37–54). Oceano Verlag.

Eisel, U. (1982). Die schöne Landschaft als kritische Utopie oder als konservatives Relikt. Über die Kristallisation gegnerischer politischer Philosophien im Symbol „Landschaft". *Soziale Welt – Zeitschrift für Sozialwissenschaftliche Forschung, 33*(2), 157–168.

Eisel, U. (2009). *Landschaft und Gesellschaft. Räumliches Denken im Visier* (Raumproduktionen: Theorie und gesellschaftliche Praxis, Bd. 5). Westfälisches Dampfboot.

Elton, S. (2019). Reconsidering the retail foodscape from a posthumanist and ecological determinants of health perspective: wading out of the food swamp. *Critical Public Health, 29*(3), 370–378. https://doi.org/10.1080/09581596.2018.1468870.

Fassmann, H. (2009). *Stadtgeographie I. Allgemeine Stadtgeographie (Das Geographische Seminar,* (2nd ed., Vol. 1). Westermann.

Giddens, A. (1984). *The constitution of society. Outline of the theory of structuration.* University of California Press.

Glasze, G., & Mattissek, A. (2009). Diskursforschung in der Humangeographie: Konzeptionelle Grundlagen und empirische Operationalisierung. In G. Glasze & A. Mattissek (Eds.), *Handbuch Diskurs und Raum. Theorien und Methoden für die Humangeographie sowie die sozial- und kulturwissenschaftliche Raumforschung* (pp. 11–59). Transcript.

Goodman, D., DuPuis, E. M., & Goodman, M. K. (2011). *Alternative food networks. Knowledge, practice, and politics.* Routledge.

Greider, T., & Garkovich, L. (1994). Landscapes: The social construction of nature and the environment. *Rural Sociology, 59*(1), 1–24. https://doi.org/10.1111/j.1549-0831.1994.tb0 0519.x.

Grell, B. (2010). „Feeding America and the World". In S. Selke (Ed.), *Kritik der Tafeln in Deutschland: Standortbestimmungen zu einem ambivalenten sozialen Phänomen* (pp. 129–146). VS Verlag. https://doi.org/10.1007/978-3-531-92611-7_6.

Grigg, D. (1995). The geography of food consumption: a review. *Progress in Human Geography, 19*(3), 338–354.

Grigg, D. (1999). The chaning geography of World food consumption in the second half of the twentieth century. *The Geographical Journal, 165*(1), 1–11.

Gruenter, R. (1975 [1953]. Landschaft. Bemerkungen zu Wort und Bedeutungsgeschichte. In A. Ritter (Ed.), *Landschaft und Raum in der Erzählkunst* (Wege der Forschung, vol. 418, pp. 192–207). WBG.

Guthman, J. (2013). Too much food and too little sidewalk? Problematizing the obesogenic environment thesis. *Environment and Planning A: Economy and Space, 45*(1), 142–158. https://doi.org/10.1068/a45130.

Hall, S. (2001). Foucault: Power, knowledge and discourse. In M. Wetherell, S. Taylor, & S. J. Yates (Eds.), *Discourse theory and practice. A reader* (pp. 72–81). SAGE Publications.

Hard, G. (1969). Das Wort Landschaft und sein semantischer Hof. Zu Methode und Ergebnis eines linguistischen Tests. *Wirkendes Wort, 19* (pp. 3–14).

Hard, G. (1977). Zu den Landschaftsbegriffen der Geographie. In A. Hartlieb von Wallthor & H. Quirin (Eds.), *„Landschaft" als interdisziplinäres Forschungsproblem. Vorträge und Diskussionen des Kolloquiums am 7./8. November 1975 in Münster* (pp. 13–24). Aschendorff.

Hartke, W. (1956). Die „Sozialbrache" als Phänomen der geographischen Differenzierung der Landschaft. *Erdkunde, 10*(4), 257–269.

Heineberg, H. (2003). *Einführung in die Anthropogeographie, Humangeographie* (Grundriss allgemeine Geographie, vol. 2445). Schöningh.

Heinritz, G., Klein, K., & Popp, M. (2003). *Geographische Handelsforschung.* Borntraeger.

Höfer, W., & Vicenzotti, V. (2013). From brownfields to postindustrial landscapes. Evolving concepts in North America and Europe. In P. Howard, I. Thompson, & E. Waterton (Eds.), *The routledge companion to landscape studies* (pp. 405–416). Routledge.

Hohl, H. (1977). Das Thema Landschaft in der deutschen Malerei des ausgehenden 18. und beginnenden 19. Jahrhunderts. In A. Hartlieb von Wallthor, & H. Quirin (Eds.), *„Landschaft" als interdisziplinäres Forschungsproblem. Vorträge und Diskussionen des Kolloquiums am 7./8. November 1975 in Münster* (pp. 45–53). Aschendorff.

Ipsen, D. (2006). *Ort und Landschaft.* VS Verlag.

Jenal, C. (2019). (Alt)Industrielandschaften. In O. Kühne, F. Weber, K. Berr, & C. Jenal (Eds.), *Handbuch Landschaft* (pp. 831–841). Springer VS.

Kersting, W. (2009). *Verteidigung des Liberalismus.* Murmann.

Kirchhoff, T. (2019). Politische Weltanschauungen und Landschaft. In O. Kühne, F. Weber, K. Berr, & C. Jenal (Eds.), *Handbuch Landschaft* (pp. 383–396). Springer VS.

Kirchhoff, T., & Trepl, L. (2001). Vom Wert der Biodiversität. Über konkurrierende politische Theorien in der Diskussion um Biodiversität. *Zeitschrift für angewandte Umweltforschung, Sonderheft, 13,* (pp. 27–44).

Kornai, J. (1980). *Economics of Shortage.* North-Holland Publications.

Kornai, J. (1992). *The socialist system. The political economy of communism.* Oxford University Press.

Kortländer, B. (1977). Die Landschaft in der Literatur des ausgehenden 18. und beginnenden 19. Jahrhunderts. In A. Hartlieb von Wallthor & H. Quirin (Eds.), *„Landschaft" als interdisziplinäres Forschungsproblem. Vorträge und Diskussionen des Kolloquiums am 7./8. November 1975 in Münster.* Aschendorff.

Krings, T. (1997). Hunger und Nahrungskrisen – ein neues Feld der wirtschaftsgeographischen Entwicklungsländerforschung – mit einer Fallstudie aus Mali/Westafrika. *Beiträge zur Bevölkerungs- und Sozialgeographie, 6,* (pp. 26–36).

Küchler, J., & Wang, X. (2009). Vielfältig und vieldeutig. Natur und Landschaft im Chinesischen. In T. Kirchhoff & L. Trepl (Eds.), *Vieldeutige Natur. Landschaft, Wildnis und Ökosystem als kulturgeschichtliche Phänomene* (Sozialtheorie, pp. 201–220). Transcript.

Kühne, O. (2002). Landwirtschaft und Arbeitslosigkeit im ländlichen Raum Polens – eine Untersuchung in Hinblick auf die EU-Osterweiterung. *Osteuropa-Wirtschaft,47*(2), 149–172).

Kühne, O. (2003). *Umwelt und Transformation in Polen. Eine kybernetisch-systemtheoretische Analyse* (Mainzer Geographische Studien, vol. 51). Geographisches Institut der Johannes Gutenberg-Universität Mainz.

Kühne, O. (2008). Die Sozialisation von Landschaft – sozialkonstruktivistische Überlegungen, empirische Befunde und Konsequenzen für den Umgang mit dem Thema Landschaft in Geographie und räumlicher Planung. *Geographische Zeitschrift,96*(4), 189–206.

Kühne, O. (2011). Die Konstruktion von Landschaft aus Perspektive des politischen Liberalismus. Zusammenhänge zwischen politischen Theorien und Umgang mit Landschaft. *Naturschutz und Landschaftsplanung,43*(6), 171–176.

Kühne, O. (2013). *Landschaftstheorie und Landschaftspraxis. Eine Einführung aus sozialkonstruktivistischer Perspektive.* Springer VS.

Kühne, O. (2015). Weltanschauungen in regionalentwickelndem Handeln – die Beispiele liberaler und konservativer Ideensysteme. In O. Kühne & F. Weber (Eds.), *Bausteine der Regionalentwicklung* (pp. 55–69). Springer VS.

Kühne, O. (2016). Transformation, Hybridisierung, Streben nach Eindeutigkeit und Urbanizing former Suburbs (URFSURBS): Entwicklungen postmoderner Stadtlandhybride in Südkalifornien und in Altindustrieäumen Mitteleuropas – Beobachtungen aus der Perspektive sozialkonstruktivistischer Landschaftsforschung. In S. Hofmeister & O. Kühne (Eds.), *StadtLandschaften. Die neue Hybridität von Stadt und Land* (pp. 13–36). Springer VS.

Kühne, O. (2018a). *Landschaftstheorie und Landschaftspraxis. Eine Einführung aus sozialkonstruktivistischer Perspektive (2., aktualisierte und* (überarbeitete). Springer VS.

Kühne, O. (2018b). Reboot „Regionale Geographie" – Ansätze einer neopragmatischen Rekonfiguration „horizontaler Geographien". *Berichte. Geographie und Landeskunde,92*(2), 101–121).

Kühne, O. (2019a). *Landscape theories. A brief introduction.* Springer VS.

Kühne, O. (2019b). Vom ‚ Bösen' und ‚ Guten' in der Landschaft – das Problem moralischer Kommunikation im Umgang mit Landschaft und ihren Konflikten. In K. Berr & C. Jenal (Eds.), *Landschaftskonflikte* (pp. 131–142). Springer VS.

Kühne, O. (2019c). Zwischen Macht und Essenz, Konstrukt und Objekt? Wie Landschaftstheorien Deutungskonkurrenzen von Natur zeigen. *Stadt+Grün,68*(12), 24–27).

Kühne, O., & Berr, K. (2021). *Wissenschaft, Raum, Gesellschaft. Eine Einführung zur sozialen Erzeugung von Wissen.* Springer VS.

Kühne, O., & Jenal, C. (2020a). *Baton Rouge – The multivillage metropolis. A neopragmatic landscape biographical approach on spatial pastiches, hybridization, and differentiation.* Springer VS.

Kühne, O., & Jenal, C. (2020b). Stadtlandhybride Prozesse in Baton Rouge: Von der klassischen Downtown zur postmodernen Downtownsimulation. In R. Duttmann, O. Kühne, & F. Weber (Eds.), *Landschaft als Prozess* (pp. 431–454). Springer VS.

Kühne, O., & Jenal, C. (2021a). Baton Rouge – A neopragmatic regional geographic approach. *Urban Science, 5*(1), 1–17. https://doi.org/10.3390/urbansci5010017.

Kühne, O., & Jenal, C. (2021b). Baton Rouge (Louisiana): On the importance of thematic cartography for 'Neopragmatic Horizontal Geography'. *KN – Journal of Cartography and Geographic Information, 71*(1), 23–31. https://doi.org/10.1007/s42489-020-00054-z.

Kühne, O., Hernik, J., & Gawroński, K. (2015). Fazit. In O. Kühne, K. Gawroński, & J. Hernik (Eds.), *Transformation und Landschaft. Die Folgen sozialer Wandlungsprozesse auf Landschaft* (pp. 339–342). Springer VS.

Kühne, O., Gawroński, K., & Hernik, J. (Eds.). (2015). *Transformation und Landschaft. Die Folgen sozialer Wandlungsprozesse auf Landschaft.* Springer VS.

Kühne, O., Jenal, C., & Koegst, L. (2020). Postmoderne Siedlungsentwicklungen in Baton Rouge, Louisiana: Stadtlandhybridität und Raumpastiches zwischen Begrenzungen und Entgrenzungen. In F. Weber, C. Wille, B. Caesar, & J. Hollstegge (Eds.), *Geographien der Grenzen. Räume – Ordnungen – Verflechtungen* (pp. 391–411). Springer VS.

Kühne, O., Berr, K., Schuster, K., & Jenal, C. (2021). *Freiheit und Landschaft. Auf der Suche nach Lebenschancen mit Ralf Dahrendorf.* Springer.

Kulke, E. (2001). Entwicklungstendenzen suburbaner Einzelhandelslandschaften. In K. Brake, J. S. Dangschat, & G. Herfert (Eds.), *Suburbanisierung in Deutschland. Aktuelle Tendenzen* (pp. 57–69). Leske+Budrich.

La polyphonie linguistique. (2009). *Langue française, 164*(4), 3–9. https://doi.org/10.3917/lf.164.0003.

Lake, A. A. (2018). Neighbourhood food environments: food choice, foodscapes and planning for health. *Proceedings of the Nutrition Society,77*(3), 239–246. https://doi.org/10.1017/S0029665118000022.

Lake, A. A., Alvanides, S., & Townshend, T. G. (Eds.). (2010). *Obesogenic environments. complexities, perceptions, and objective measures.* Wiley-Blackwell.

Langhagen-Rohrbach, C. (2010). *Raumordnung und Raumplanung.* 2. Aufl. (Geowissen kompakt). WBG.

Latour, B. (1996). *Petite réflexion sur le culte moderne des dieux Faitiches.* Synthélabo groupe.

Latour, B. (1997). The Trouble with Actor-Network Theory. *Soziale Welt – Zeitschrift für Sozialwissenschaftliche Forschung,47,* (369–381).

Latour, B., & Roßler, G. (2007 [2005]). *Eine neue Soziologie für eine neue Gesellschaft. Einführung in die Akteur-Netzwerk-Theorie.* Suhrkamp.

Lautensach, H. (1973). Über die Erfassung und Abgrenzung von Landschaftsräumen [Erstveröffentlichung 1938]. In K. Paffen (Ed.), *Das Wesen der Landschaft* (Wege der Forschung, vol. 39, pp. 20–38). WBG.

Leibenath, M., & Otto, A. (2013). Windräder in Wolfhagen – eine Fallstudie zur diskursiven Konstituierung von Landschaften. In M. Leibenath, S. Heiland, H. Kilper, & S.

Tzschaschel (Eds.), *Wie werden Landschaften gemacht? Sozialwissenschaftliche Perspektiven auf die Konstituierung von Kulturlandschaften* (pp. 205–236). Transcript.

Lekan, T., & Zeller, T. (2005). The landscape of German environmental history. In T. Lekan & T. Zeller (Eds.), *Germany's Nature. Cultural Landscapes and Environmental History* (pp. 1–16). Rutgers University Press.

Lévi-Strauss, C., & Moldenhauer, E. (1976). *Das Rohe und das Gekochte (Suhrkamp-Taschenbuch Wissenschaft,* (1st ed., Vol. 167). Suhrkamp.

Lohnert, B. (1995). *Überleben am Rande der Stadt. Ernährungssicherungspolitik, Getreidehandel und verwundbare Gruppen in Mali ; das Beispiel Mopti* (Freiburger Studien zur geographischen Entwicklungsforschung, vol. 8). Verlag für Entwicklungspolitik (Zugl.: Freiburg (Breisgau), Univ., Diss., 1994).

Luhmann, N. (1986). *Ökologische Kommunikation. Kann die moderne Gesellschaft sich auf ökologische Gefährdungen einstellen?* Westdeutscher Verlag.

Maar, K. (2010). Tafeln aus der Perspektive der sozialpädagogischen NutzerInnenforschung. In S. Selke (Ed.), *Kritik der Tafeln in Deutschland: Standortbestimmungen zu einem ambivalenten sozialen Phänomen* (pp. 233–239). VS Verlag.

MacKendrick, N. (2014). Foodscape. *Contexts, 13*(3), 16–18. https://doi.org/10.1177/153650 4214545754.

Marx, K. (2014 [1872]). *Das Kapital. Kritik der politischen Ökonomie* (Ungekürzte Ausgabe nach der 2. Aufl. 1872). Nikol.

Miewald, C., & McCann, E. (2014). Foodscapes and the geographies of poverty: Sustenance, strategy, and politics in an Urban neighborhood. *Antipode, 46*(2), 537–556). https://doi. org/10.1111/anti.12057.

Minaker, L. M. (2016). Retail food environments in Canada: Maximizing the impact of research, policy and practice. *Canadian journal of public health = Revue canadienne de sante publique, 107*(1), 1–3. https://doi.org/10.17269/cjph.107.5632.

Molling, L. (2009). Die Berliner Tafel zwischen Sozialstaatsabbau und neuer Armenfürsorge. In S. Selke (Ed.), *Tafeln in Deutschland: Aspekte einer sozialen Bewegung zwischen Nahrungsmittelumverteilung und Armutsintervention* (pp. 175–196). VS Verlag.

Morton, L. W., & Blanchard, T. C. (2007). Starved for Access: Life in Rural America's Food Deserts. *Rural Realities, 1*(4), 1–10.

Müller, G. (1977). Zur Geschichte des Wortes Landschaft. In A. Hartlieb von Wallthor & H. Quirin (Eds.), *„Landschaft" als interdisziplinäres Forschungsproblem. Vorträge und Diskussionen des Kolloquiums am 7./8. November 1975 in Münster* (pp. 3–13). Aschendorff.

Müller, M. (2015). Assemblages and actor-networks: Rethinking socio-material power, politics and space. *Geography Compass, 9*(1), 27–41). https://doi.org/10.1111/gec3.12192.

Niles, D., & Roff, R. J. (2008). Shifting agrifood systems: the contemporary geography of food and agriculture; an introduction. *GeoJournal, 73*(1), 1–10. https://doi.org/10.1007/ s10708-008-9174-4.

Normann, K. von. (2009). Ernährungsarmut und „Tafelarbeit" in Deutschland. Distributionspolitische Hintergründe und nonprofit-basierte Lösungsstrategien. In S. Selke (Ed.), *Tafeln in Deutschland: Aspekte einer sozialen Bewegung zwischen Nahrungsmittelumverteilung und Armutsintervention* (pp. 85–106). VS Verlag.

Otremba, E. (1953). *Allgemeine Agrar- und Industriegeographie* (Erde und Weltwirtschaft, vol. 3). Franckh'sche Verlagshandlung W. Keller & Co.

Palm, F. (2021). Verwirklichungschancen und Mobilität in Baton Rouge. Eine Annäherung auf Grundlage Amartya Sens Capability-Ansatz. In O. Kühne, T. Sedelmeier, & C. Jenal (Eds.), *Louisiana – mediengeographische Beiträge zu einer neopragmatischen Regionalen Geographie* (p. xx). Springer (im Druck).

Piepmeier, R. (1980). Das Ende der ästhetischen Kategorie „Landschaft". Zu einem Aspekt neuzeitlichen Naturverhältnisses. *Westfälische Forschungen – Zeitschrift des Westfälischen Instituts für Regionalgeschichte des Landschaftsverbandes Westfalen-Lippe, 30,* (pp. 8–46).

Popper, K. R. (2003[1945]). *Die offene Gesellschaft und ihre Feinde. Bd. 1: Der Zauber Platons* (8. Aufl.). Mohr Siebeck.

Rawls, J. (1993). *Political liberalism.* Columbia University Press.

Rivera López, E. (1995). *Die moralischen Voraussetzungen des Liberalismus.* Alber.

Rothstein, B. (2001). Social capital in the social democratic welfare State. *Politics & Society, 29*(2), 207–241. https://doi.org/10.1177/0032329201029002003.

Ruppert, K. (1984). Agrargeographie im Wandel. *Geographica Helvetica, 39*(4), 168–172.

Scharpf, F. W., & (1998,. (1996). Negative and positive integration in the political economy of European welfare states. In G. Marks, F. W. Scharpf, P. C. Schmitter, & W. Streeck (Eds.), *Governance in the European union* (pp. 15–39). SAGE Publications.

Schenk, W. (2013). Landschaft als zweifache sekundäre Bildung – historische Aspekte im aktuellen Gebrauch von Landschaft im deutschsprachigen Raum, namentlich in der Geographie. In D. Bruns & O. Kühne (Eds.), *Landschaften: Theorie, Praxis und internationale Bezüge. Impulse zum Landschaftsbegriff mit seinen ästhetischen, ökonomischen, sozialen und philosophischen Bezügen mit dem Ziel, die Verbindung von Theorie und Planungspraxis zu stärken* (pp. 23–36). Oceano Verlag.

Schmithüsen, J. (1968). Der wissenschaftliche Landschaftsbegriff. In R. Tüxen (Ed.), *Pflanzensoziologie und Landschaftsökologie (Berichte über die Internationalen Symposia der Internationalen Vereinigung für Vegetationskunde* (Vol. 7, pp. 9–19). Springer.

Schönwald, A. (2015). Die Transformation von Altindustrielandschaften zwischen Kontinuität und Wandel. In O. Kühne, K. Gawroński, & J. Hernik (Eds.), *Transformation und Landschaft. Die Folgen sozialer Wandlungsprozesse auf Landschaft* (pp. 63–73). Springer VS.

Schultze, J. H. (1973). Landschaft (1966/70). In K. Paffen (Ed.), *Das Wesen der Landschaft* (Wege der Forschung, vol. 39, pp. 202–222). WBG.

Schulz-Schaeffer, I. (2000). Akteur-Netzwerk-Theorie: Zur Koevolution von Gesellschaft, Natur und Technik. In J. Weyer & J. Abel (Eds.), *Soziale Netzwerke. Konzepte und Methoden der sozialwissenschaftlichen Netzwerkforschung* (Lehr- und Handbücher der Soziologie, pp. 187–210). Oldenbourg Wissenschaftsverlag.

Sedelmeier, T. (2011). *Armut und Ernährung in Deutschland. Eine Untersuchung zur Rolle und Wirksamkeit der Tafeln bei der Lebensmittelausgabe an Bedürftige.* Mensch und Buch (Zugl.: Freiburg, Univ., Diss., 2011).

Sedelmeier, T. (2013). Süddeutschland ist »Tafelland«. Eine Analyse der räumlichen Diskrepanz zwischen Angebot und Bedarf der Lebensmittel-Tafeln. *Ethik und Gesellschaft,* (1), 1–18. https://doi.org/10.18156/EUG-1-2013-ART-6.

Sedelmeier, T. (2018). Urbane Nahrungslandschaften – ungleicher Zugang zu Nahrungsmitteln. *Berichte. Geographie und Landeskunde, 92*(3–4), 267–277.

Sedelmeier, T. (2019). Food Deserts – Einblicke in Nahrungslandschaften. In K. Berr & C. Jenal (Eds.), *Landschaftskonflikte* (pp. 687–698). Springer VS.

Segbers, F. (2011). Pflaster auf eine Wunde, die zu groß ist. Tafeln, Sozialkaufhäuser und andere Dienste zwischen Armutslinderung und Armutsüberwindung. In J. Eurich, F. Barth, K. Baumann, & G. Wegner (Eds.), *Kirchen aktiv gegen Armut und Ausgrenzung. Theologische Grundlagen und praktische Ansätze für Diakonie und Gemeinde* (pp. 475–492). Kohlhammer.

Selke, S. (2009). *Fast ganz unten. Wie man in Deutschland durch die Hilfe von Lebensmitteltafeln satt wird* (2nd ed.). Westfälisches Dampfboot.

Selke, S. (2014). *Lifelogging. Wie die digitale Selbstvermessung unsere Gesellschaft verändert*. Econ.

Sen, A. (1982). *Choice, welfare and measurement*. Blackwell Publishers.

Sen, A. (1985). *Commodities and capabilities*. North-Holland Publications.

Shannon, J. (2014). Food deserts: Governing obesity in the neoliberal city. *Progress in Human Geography,38*(2), 248–266.

Shaw, H. J. (2006). Food deserts: Towards the development of a classification. *Geografiska Annaler: Series B, Human Geography,88*(2), 231–247.

Sick, W.-D. (1983). *Agrargeographie (Das Geographische Seminar)*. Westermann.

Smith, D. M. (1996). The socialist city. In G. D. Andrusz, I. Szelényi, & M. Harloe (Eds.), *Cities after Socialism. Urban and Regional Change and Conflict in Post-Socialist Societies* (pp. 286–317). Blackwell Publishers.

Sperk, C., & Kistemann, T. (2012). Food desert oder gesunde Stadt? Eine Untersuchung von Nahrungslandschaften in Bonn. *Berichte zur deutschen Landeskunde,86*(2), 135–151.

Tilley, C. (1997). *A phenomenology of landscape. Places, paths and monuments* (Explorations in anthropology). Berg.

Trepl, L. (2012). *Die Idee der Landschaft. Eine Kulturgeschichte von der Aufklärung bis zur Ökologiebewegung*. Transcript.

Tröger, S. (2004). *Handeln zur Ernährungssicherung im Zeichen gesellschaftlichen Umbruchs. Untersuchungen auf dem Ufipa-Plateau im Südwesten Tansanias* (Studien zur Geographischen Entwicklungsforschung, vol. 27). Verlag für Entwicklungspolitik.

Troll, C. (1939). Luftbildplan und ökologische Bodenforschung. Ihr zweckmäßiger Einsatz für die wissenschaftliche Erforschung und praktische Erschließung wenig bekannter Länder. *Zeitschrift der Gesellschaft für Erdkunde zu Berlin*, (7–8), 241–298.

Tuan, Y.-F. (1989). Surface phenomena and aesthetic experience. *Annals of the Association of American Geographers,79*(2), 233–241. https://doi.org/10.1111/j.1467-8306.1989.tb0 0260.x.

Ueda, H. (2010). A study on residential landscape perception through landscape Image. Four case studies in German and Japanese Rural Communities. (Inaugural Dissertation). Kassel. https://kobra.bibliothek.uni-kassel.de/bitstream/urn:nbn:de:hebis:34-200 9072029116/3/ThesisHirofumiUeda.pdf. Accessed: 26 Apr 2017.

van Wezemael, J., & Loepfe, M. (2009). Veränderte Prozesse der Entscheidungsfindung in der Raumentwicklung. *Geographica Helvetica,64*(2), 106–118.

Vicenzotti, V. (2011). *Der »Zwischenstadt«-Diskurs. Eine Analyse zwischen Wildnis, Kulturlandschaft und Stadt*. Transcript.

Vonthron, S., Perrin, C., & Soulard, C.-T. (2020). Foodscape: A scoping review and a research agenda for food security-related studies. *PloS one,15*(5), 1–26. https://doi.org/10.1371/journal.pone.0233218.

Wakefield, S., Fleming, J., Klassen, C., & Skinner, A. (2012). Sweet Charity, revisited: Organizational responses to food insecurity in Hamilton and Toronto, Canada. *Critical Social Policy,33*(3), 427–450. https://doi.org/10.1177/0261018312458487.

Warshawsky, D. N. (2010). New power relations served here: The growth of food banking in Chicago. *Geoforum,41*(5), 763–775. https://doi.org/10.1016/j.geoforum.2010.04.008.

Weber, F. (2019). Landschaftskonflikte' aus poststrukturalistisch-diskurstheoretischer Perspektive. In K. Berr & C. Jenal (Eds.), *Landschaftskonflikte* (pp. 51–64). Springer VS.

Whatmore, S., Stassart, P., & Renting, H. (2003). What's Alternative about alternative food networks? *Environment and Planning A,35*(3), 389–391. https://doi.org/10.1068/a3621.

Winchester, H. P. M., Kong, L., & Dunn, K. (2003). *Landscapes. Ways of imagining the world.* Routledge.

Wolff, M. (2016). Was bringen die Tafeln? Eine kritische Betrachtung aus Nutzer-Perspektive. *Ethik und Gesellschaft*, (2), 1–18. https://doi.org/10.18156/EUG-2-2016-ART-8.

Wright, J. D., Donley, A. M., Gualtieri, M. C., & Strickhouser, S. M. (2016). Food deserts: What is the problem? What is the solution? *Society, 53*(2), 171–181. https://doi.org/10.1007/s12115-016-9993-8.

Wylie, J. (2007). *Landscape.* Routledge.

Yasmeen, G. (1996). Bangkok's foodscape : public eating, gender relations and urban change. (Dissertation, University of British Columbia). Vancouver. https://open.library.ubc.ca/cIRcle/collections/ubctheses/831/items/1.0088160. Accessed: 30 Mar 2021.

Printed in the United States
by Baker & Taylor Publisher Services